# Secrets in Anderton Forest

## An Extraordinary General Meeting

*Book One of The Secrets in Anderton Forest Series.*

Author: A. Daly

Dedicated to:

All you young readers everywhere
who dare to believe that magic exists in every forest
—

And just like the families, creatures, and beings who
live there —
may you grow to support and protect one another,

nature, and this world.

And maybe — just maybe —
you'll accidentally find
your own forest meeting.

- A.D.

A portion of the proceeds from this book is donated to the Woodland Trust, supporting the protection and restoration of native forests. To learn more about trees, wildlife, and how to care for our forests, visit:

woodlandtrust.org.uk
crann.ie

# Anderton Forest Map – 1852

**B.G's Family** - have always lived in Moss Folly

**Oldfather** - The Wizard - lives in Tawney place where he looks after the library and guards the Wisdom Book of Records for Anderton Forest.

**Doeity**,. the deer & Stag hang out in the Heathlands

**Quillton** - The Rook who "beak writes" has his nest with the others in Rooks Canopy.

**Higginbottom** - Lives in The Haggart, near The Edgelands.   *-A.D.*

# Anderton Forest Guardians

1. **B.G**. - 2. **Doeity** – 3. **Quillton** - 4. **Oldfather**

# The Main Characters

1. **The Lady.** - 2. **B.G. In Riverfalls.** - 3. **Doeity in The Heathlands.** 4. - **Quillton chatting.** 5.- **Oldfather in his library.** 6. **Higginbottom – The Farmer.**

# The Lady

## *An Office Manager*

The lady works in a busy London office. She moved there when she was young to be near her Aunt, when her Mother passed.

During an unplanned visit to Anderton Forest, she discovers she has a deep connection with this magical place.

She has always felt that woodlands and forests should be protected now more than ever.

Her accidental encounter in Anderton Forest leaves her with more questions than answers.

She thinks its just a spiritual connection from her visit, however, she has no idea what will unfold............ but the Book of Wisdom does.

# B.G.

## *Guardian & Gatekeeper of Anderton Forest*

B.G wears his family crest with pride. He takes his role as Gatekeeper of Anderton Forest very seriously attending to every detail, just like his Father, Great-grandfather and past generations.

His Great-grandfather got honoured in the Book of Wisdom for bravery in risking his life for others, and it is B.G`.s silent wish to follow in his footsteps.

He can be impatient at times, but he has a big heart. Likes to dress well and occasionally uses his pocket handkerchief, or indeed his blue cap, to send secret messages on occasion.

## *Doeity*

### Guardian of Anderton Forest

Doeity loves roaming free on the Heathlands with the deer and stag. She is very gentle and kind.

When she lost her husband, to Farmer Higginbottoms wicked ways, she became close friends with B.G.

Sometimes they go for walks together with B.G. perched on her back for a better view, while they chatter about all the forest stories.

She is cared for by everyone and feels that everyone is her family now.

# Quillton

## *Guardian & Beak-writer*

Quillton is a beak-writer and he writes the notes for the meetings with his beak on bark wood with natural ink from the forest.

His great grandmother invented the art of beak writing and it stayed with the family ever since.

Quillton is a bit of a joker and doesn't like working very much, especially building nests.

He hurt his leg years ago and walks with a limp occasionally - more noticeable during nest building season.

He almost lost the beak-writing skill years ago, but with B.G.`s help and mentorship, he now feels he does a good job. He can get himself covered in ink sometimes, which amuses everyone, but he is valued by all now.

# Oldfather Owl

## *Guardian & Wizard*

Oldfather lives with his wife in Tawney Dale. He comes from a family of good wisdom wizardry and all his Forefathers were writers and designers of magic and were very intelligent. He takes great pride in guarding all the old books and records of Anderton Forest.

The oldest dates back to 1756, titled The Wisdom Book of Magic. Occasionally, the book will record deeds of outstanding bravery and it is a great honour when this occurs. Its kept safe under lock and key by Oldfather in his library. He is a wise fellow and likes his quiet home. He wears glasses when reading and speaks with a deep voice and is respected by all.

# Mr. Higginbottom

## *Farmer in The Edgelands*

Higginbottom lives in The Haggart close to the Edgelands. He came over from Ireland about 20 years ago. He is a bit of a scrooge and lives alone.

.The creatures of Anderton Forest have to be on the look out for him at all times. He doesn't like animals and prefers his red Massey Tractor over any kind of car. Occasionally, he travels down to the local town for food.

Even though he knows Anderton Forest is preserved, he still cuts down the trees — unseen he thinks — but not quite.

A few locals have warned him, but he doesn't listen to them. On the other hand, he loves rabbit stew (unfortunately).

# Anderton Forest

It was a wonderful sunny morning. The lady had enjoyed being out exploring the beach and collecting shells for her artwork. Driving back to the hotel, through the car window, she saw a sign for Anderton Forest and felt an immediate urge to visit it at that moment in time. Well... this part of England was new to her and she was curious, so she turned left and drove on and on, but where was it?. She had been driving for what seemed like ages without any signs or directions and she really wanted to take a forest walk. Trees are magical and not everyone notices this, she thought. She continued driving until, eventually coming to an entrance sign for parking and parked her car and got out .Taking a big deep breath of the fresh country air, while grabbing her binoculars she set off.

It was a wonderful day and the stillness of the forest was something quite different to the city life she was used to, with all its noise and smells. I think it was good for her to have time out to enjoy this trip. The receptionist in the hotel had said that, if she was going to visit the forest to stay on the outer path only and when she asked her why, she just smiled and said, "some stories have been told about strange things going on there, but no one knows for sure what it is, so it's best to be careful. She was now more curious than ever and after all, she was on holiday.

There was a very large blue sign showing the pathways people should take with various points marked out along the route. There was also a little history. Apparently it was one of the second oldest in England after Cherrywood Forest. She wondered if famous people had visited there in times gone by. Anyhow, she decided to walk on into the forest, without following any particular route. It was the month of June, and under rows and rows of tall trees were beautiful wild-flowers, white yellow and purple stretched out in front of her as far as the eye could see on various bushes and pathways.

Surrounded by so many wonderful shades of green. It was, she thought, just the best way to welcome an arrival into this magical forest and mother nature had designed it picture perfect for this day.

As she walked along the forest paths, chirping birds echoed here and there as they excitedly played hide and seek calling out to each other through the green bushes and branches. The sun shone down through the trees above her head and she could see lots of rooks nests perched here and there among the tree top branches. Their babies had been born by this time and were probably enjoying the sunshine too. She could hear them calling each other in the distance. Some bumble bees were buzzing around here and there looking for nectar deep in the flowers. Various paths led the way forward, created by forest animals and perhaps a few visitors. Some of the paths were a little overgrown but she was still able to get through by pushing the branches out of her way. On and on she walked for what seemed like a long time enjoying everything and, indeed, it was so nice to forget all about the time and just wander along enjoying the view, the smells and sounds of the sunny forest. Coming across a stream which flowed down alongside the small path she was walking along. As it twisted and turned here and there,it was a guide for her just in case she got lost.

Then unexpectedly, she discovered a clearing right in the middle, a flat area in the forest. Unusually there were no trees growing here. Smiling to herself she felt lost in nature and away from all distractions.

The open area was a circular open area filled with tiny worn paths, made by small and large forest animals among the rich green grasses, flowers and a few small bushes grew here and there.

   She had walked for some hours before discovering this special place right in the middle of the forest. There were many small paths made by forest animals who visited this place. Here and there among the rich green grasses were flowers and a few small bushes.

   She had a feeling that somehow this was a special place, she couldn't say exactly why, but it was just a feeling that came to her from the moment she arrived there. At the other end of this open area was a rather large green tree stump, weathered by time and covered with some moss and also had some ivy growing over it. Over to the right there was a huge oak tree with large branches reaching out towards her.

Getting closer, she realized this was not an ordinary oak tree. The trunk had a rather large curved shape that looked just like an old armchair built into its large trunk and with two curved armrests jutting out of it.

   It was partially hidden by a large green bush covered in yellow flowers. The seat shaped tree trunk was facing out towards this green grassy area with its many criss-crossed paths lined with brightly coloured wild flowers. It was a magical place and the strange thing was she felt that this tree was calling her to sit there and to rest for a while, and so she did.

After walking for a few hours she was tired. Placing her binoculars on her lap, she stretched out her legs, leaned back on this seat and looked upwards to the sky, which was a perfect blue with just a few white clouds peeking out over the tallest green tree tops. She closed her eyes, smiling for a few seconds while listening to the birds singing.

Now did she fall asleep? I am not entirely sure. Was she sitting on a magical throne, who knows? But, from the very moment she listened to the birds, she could also hear animal noises and there was an excited chatter taking place . Over to her right side was a noisy group of rabbits, yes rabbits. She just couldn't believe it. They were all shapes and sizes, big ones, small ones, Mummies, Daddies, all making their way into the clearing.

*Rabbits Playing*

Many of the babies ran around excitedly playing hide and seek among the tall green grasses and yellow buttercups while having lots and lots of fun, in fact, one almost came over to where she was resting. The babies were running around trying to catch each other's tails and It was a wonderful sight.

Even more surprising was when so many other animals and birds arrived. Pigeons, rooks and squirrels were taking

their place among the branches of the trees and a rustling noise came from somewhere behind the trees at the edge of the clearing. They came from far and wide to listen to the Forest Guardians.

# An Extraordinary General Meeting

Suddenly all the noises stopped and just then, astonishingly she heard a voice….."This is the 22$^{nd}$ extraordinary general meeting called by me, the gatekeeper of Anderton Forest" said a rather large sprightly rabbit standing on the old tree stump, she could see from her binoculars that he was looking over his notepad while trying to check his watch at the same time. He was smartly dressed with a bright blue jacket and matching cap.

He looked out over all the other rabbits and woodland creatures who were now standing side by side listening to what he had to say. By this time many more woodland animals had arrived and the trees were alive with pigeons, squirrels and rooks all excitedly looking around.

Even a deer had poked its nose out from the surrounding trees. Two lazy overweight badgers poked their heads out from their den not far from where she sat.

They were lucky they didn't have to travel far, but they didn't notice her at all; they seemed to be ignoring everything else except B.G. The gatekeeper of Anderton Forest and what he was saying.

On a branch behind the tree stump, where the rabbit stood, was a black rook. He was busy taking the notes of the meeting. He was beak writing onto the inside of a piece of bark, while occasionally dipping his beak into a black liquid. She was trying hard to make out the chattering from the trees when suddenly the forest chatter stopped silent and I wondered why.

Thank goodness the rabbit speaker didn't notice her sitting in the tree armchair. She was trying to be as quiet as possible while hiding partly out of sight behind the large bush close by. To upset their meeting would have been wrong she thought. Just then the sound twigs breaking at the edge of the clearing came from over to her left. She could see the shadows of a small herd of deer through the trees. One of them stepped out gracefully from the edge of the forest clearing and and walked slowly over to the old tree stump where the gatekeeper rabbit was excitedly shuffling from one leg to the other.

"Ohhh just in time, said the rabbit as he caught sight of her. Hello B.G said to the female deer in a very soft gentle smiling voice. We are here to help too, she said. Thank you Doeity, B.G the gatekeeper rabbit replied, I knew I could count on you. With that Doeity lowered her head and B.G. skipped off the tree stump over her head and up onto her back for a better view of everyone. They must be old friends, she thought. Through her binoculars, she could just make out his family crest on his blue jacket, B.G., British Giant Rabbit family. She almost fell off my seat with excitement. And so, the rabbit continued…. "We are gathered here today to discuss the Blanc de Bouse rabbit family who are in very grave danger, " he said. Their home, in the south east part of the forest, may be lost and the De Bouse family has lived there for many many years. It lies in the path of destruction being carried out by our arch enemy Mr. Higgingbottom. For the past two days he has been cutting through the scrub and has now started cutting down some of the larger trees near to their home. Two baby rabbits were killed by a fallen tree already and I have visited the family who are totally heartbroken by their loss. The woodland community there are all horrified and I know all of you are here too.

As you may know Bell de Bouse is part of one of the oldest rabbit families here in Anderton Forest and is one of my dear friends. She is due to have her babies soon so this is indeed a crisis. She hasn't been able to sleep a wink since he started cutting down the trees. Their home will be destroyed and they have spent so much time preparing it for their new family due to arrive any day now. Their underground tunnels from their home at the bottom of their tree trunk connecting with their neighbours may also be destroyed, so we have got to act fast. I have asked the rooks to remain on lookout duty on this matter and they say that many other families will also be affected, including the red squirrels who live in one of the largest trees in Mr. Higginbottom`s path.

At this point the rooks and pigeons had settled in the surrounding trees and many squirrels were also standing up to attention here and there from the branches, while still chewing some nuts held tightly in their front paws. Higginbottom knows this is a protected forest B.G. continued and he should not be cutting down good trees and destroying our homes. That man has been sneaking around our forest up to no good for too long and he must be stopped. As you all know he carries a rifle that has scared many of us. Some of you already know that Benjamin Badger refuses to leave his home and is too scared to even go out for a walk ever since Higginbottom tried to catch him last month. We must stop him, and Doeity nodding her head in agreement.

"What can we do?" asked B.G". as he twitched his nose nervously looking around. There was a lot of chattering among everyone in the clearing, then a strong voice said, "We should ask the Oldfather Owl to use his wisdom book of magic". It came from one stag from the back of the herd. At this point everyone looked around and started nodding and mumbling their agreement including the herd of deer who were now stepping out into the clearing together. "Good idea",said B.G. He turned around to the rook, "can you write that in your notes Quillton", he said. Quillton`s beak was now covered in the black inky liquid at this time.

B.G. continued "You know that Oldfather Owl can only use his wisdom book of magic three times each year, but I agree, this is a crisis. As you may know, his magic book was handed down by many previous generations of Oldfather`s family and it holds the records of all the past happenings and magical affairs of Anderton Forest over hundreds of years. It is one of the most treasured possessions in Oldfather`s care in Anderton's library and we need to consult him as soon as possible and ask for his advice.

I acknowledge all your agreements B.G. the Rabbit said, while looking around at all the animals and gazing around the tree branches and everyone nodded in agreement. The rook behind him was very busy writing all for the records of the meeting. We have little time to lose, B.G. said, so, Doeity and I will visit Oldfather tonight in the deep core of the forest where he lives to get his advice. Some of the stags will be our guides along the way and Doeity will join me too and again she nodded in agreement. The fireflies will guide us because some of the paths are dangerous closer to the forest core, he said. "We must come up with a plan to stop the destruction of our trees without delay". Doeity also nodded in agreement. "If we don't do something many more lives and homes will be lost and our environment will be at risk, B.G. said. We need our forests to survive and to protect all of us who live here.

We must get his advice as quickly as possible", he said worriedly.

"We don't know how many trees Higginbottom will cut down and our families and livelihoods are in grave danger. You will all remember we have already lost two homes because of this man and you all remember last year Doeity lost her husband when Higginbottom was shooting his rifle in the forest", he said. With her binoculars she looked at Doeity through the bush and she looked so very sad from that memory and so did everyone else.

"The time has come for action", said B.G. as he raised his clenched paw in the air. "We must stop him now". Everyone nodded their heads in agreement, including Doeity.

"Now this is important" said B.G. "We will all gather back here tomorrow at the same time, to discuss Oldfather`s advice, so until then, be careful and watch out for Higginbottom". The rooks will be our eyes and ears and will pass on any important messages.

B.G. then folded his notes and the meeting ended, much to the relief of the exhausted rook taking the notes, who was now cleaning his beak off against the moss on the tree stump. Two rooks flew off then and everyone started to leave in different directions until finally they had all disappeared including the two lazy badgers. Perhaps they had disappeared into their den for a nap. She got up from her seat, stretched and pinched herself really hard to see if she was dreaming, it did hurt — "I can't be dreaming," she said.. surely not.

Feeling surprised, she looked around. The forest was now so quiet with just a few natural sounds of birds in the distance and some buzzing bees carrying out their normal life duties. Some beautiful white butterflies danced around the blossoms here and there on the bush in front of her. She could hardly believe her eyes and ears, looking at the large throne-like seat in the tree she had sat on, and wondering if it was a magical door to woodland life.

Then following the central pathway out of the open clearing she continued her way back through the forest and back to the car, hoping not to get lost. She couldn't believe what had just happened. It was now late evening and she wanted to return to the hotel but vowed to come back and find out what the plan was.

## A Sleepless Night

That night she couldn't sleep twisting and turning in her bed, unable to forget what happened in Anderton Forest while wondering what would happen next. Would B.G. and Doeity find Oldfather Owl in time and would they be able to form a plan to stop the trees being lost, animals being killed and thousands of wildlife homes being destroyed. How did she get to hear them talking and to see all that had happened at that extraordinary general meeting.

Still wondering if she had entered a magic gateway to all things mystical in Anderton forest, would It happen again and would she hear them speaking again?. She simply had no idea for sure, but she wanted to return for sure.

The night was long, and it was hard to sleep because of the excitement. The wind blew hard during the night and she fell asleep listening to branches tapping on her bedroom window in the wind. In her dreams, she saw B.G. and Doeity and their group in the forest on their way to the forest core where Oldfather lived. She saw the stags and many fireflies guiding them along in the darkness of the night. They were like hundreds of stars dancing around them. Quillton was with them keeping a look out for any danger. Doeity was with B.G. The Stag were in front with the fireflies.

It all looked so magical as they travelled through the forest. B.G. Travelled on Doeity`s back and the chatted about all the forest things. Then later she saw Oldfather`s magic book glowing in a large library in the treehouse.

In her dream she saw them all arriving at Oldfather`s home in the middle of the forest core. They chatted to each other as they travelled.

But, she could not see Oldfather in the dream. She saw

21

B.G. and Doeity trying to find him, but he was not there, there was no one home at Oldfather`s home in the forest core. They called and called for Olfather, but he did not answer. They were getting very worried. At this point, she woke up and realised she was just dreaming, which was indeed a relief.

  The morning sun was now shining in through the bedroom window. It was going to be lovely sunny day again and yet her mind was full of unanswered questions. She got up early for breakfast. The hotel was quiet as it was located in a remote part of the country. The hotel receptionist had said Anderton Forest was one of the largest in England and if she was going up there she should take a map and stay on the outer paths. She thanked her. She thought it better not to tell her about what happened the previous day, at least until she knew more. Her curiosity had peaked, and she knew she had to return because she had so many more questions that were unanswered.

  And so at exactly 12 am that morning she followed the same pathways back through the forest and eventually after some hours, arrived at the same clearing as before. The creeks of the tall trees and birds chirping here and there were the only sounds.

  Making her way over to the seat in the trunk of the large tree at the north side of the clearing she sat down again hidden by the flowery bush. She waited quietly, but nothing happened. It was all peaceful except for a rather large black and yellow bumble bee buzzing around some bright yellow flowers which took up his entire attention. Was she too late,

felling worried, she wondered if she had missed their

meeting? or maybe the meeting was over?

She closed her eyes to concentrate better on the sounds of the forest hoping to hear something and sure enough just as she did, again she heard noises from a large congregation of rabbits arriving from the right side of the clearing and lots of rabbit families, small families and big families, lots of baby bunnies, and little by little, the clearing came alive with all the forest creatures again.

The trees were full of life with all the birds, from pigeons to robins, rooks and a few more squirrels than before and all the woodland creatures were chattering away among themselves. Baby rabbits were playing here and there and rolling about among the blue and yellow flowers along the paths. After a little time passed, B.G. the gatekeeper arrived. He was smiling this time as he jumped up onto the tree stump, he seemed much happier today than he was yesterday. The plan to save the forest had begun, she thought to herself. He wore the same blue jacket and blue cap as before. B.G. looked around, straightened his jacket, smoothed his whiskers and searched in his pocket where he took out his notebook.

He glanced behind him to check on Quillton to make sure he was ready and nodded. Then sure enough Doeity the deer arrived over, smiled at him and kindly lowered her head. With a hop skip and a jump he left the tree stump and was up on her back again. He straightened his blue cap which almost fell off his head. The rook settled himself beside B.G. On the tree stump he readied himself for his writing task, this time assisted by another rook perched on top of a pile of clean bark writing materials beside a silver pot of writing ink. Then B.G. straightened his whiskers and with a short cough he started to speak to everyone there.

## Oldfather's Plan

"We have a plan" he said, "Doeity and I have been up all night with Oldfather Owl and he has consulted his wisdom magic book and has been able to give us some magic help for this horrible crisis. I want to give special thanks to the fireflies and the stags for helping us to get to the forest core. The rooks, our lookouts, have advised me that two more trees were cut down by Higginbottom yesterday and the residents there are horrified and so he needs to be stopped today. Lots of families are being affected. The Angora rabbit family are now homeless and they have young babies too.

The rooks, our lookouts, heard that he is planning to come back at 6pm this evening in his red tractor to cut more trees, so this certainly needs Oldfather's magical efforts, who was very kind to come back with us to speak to you all because he understands the crisis and how important this is to us all. He should be resting, since he has been up all night working hard too, he has kindly offered to tell you all about his plan to stop Higginbottom in his tracks. Then B.G. said, now over to you Oldfather Owl" and everyone looked up over his head as Oldfather stepped out from one of the branches above B.G.

"Greetings my friends and fellow woodlanders and thank you B.G"., said Oldfather Owl,

He spoke in a very deep and intelligent voice, as most wizards do.

"As you all know our trees are sacred in this forest of ours, he continued. We need them for shade, sun and shelter from cold and wet weather and to make our homes in them and to protect our communities and save our livelihoods and that of all the living in Anderton Forest.

The recent loss of trees has affected over four million types of life forms not to mention the sad loss of some of our friends, whom I know you miss and will remember them in your hearts. Remember by saving our trees you are saving our world so that trees can continue to reduce the poison gas called carbon, this is their job to do as Mother Earth commands and as those before us have done, so we must also", said Oldfather Owl.

He was very wise and he obviously loved passing on

important information about the forest to everyone. "I agree this is a crisis situation", Oldfather said ,"and we can

not and will not have our woodland communities affected by this bad man. So, without further delay here is the plan he said, clearing his throat, while he checked some papers he had tucked under his wing for safe keeping.

" Overnight, and with the help of my forest friends, I have prepared eight containers of magic dust. This magic dust will make you invisible to Mr. Higgingbottom and the humans, but it will only work for two hours once the containers are opened, so you must all remember this. It is very important". "After two hours it will stop working" he said. So this is what we plan to do, the rooks and pigeons will drop the magic dust over you including Doeity and her herd of deer You will then all become invisible to humans for two hours. No dust must fall on the antlers or heads of the male deer or Doeity, so that only their heads remain visible to the man. The plan is to scare Higginbottom away for good and as soon as he arrives this evening at six pm, we will attack.

The deer will jump over him and kick his tree cutting machine making loud noises which will confuse him, he pointed his wing over to the herd of deer all nodding in unison. The male deer will attack by jumping over him with their antlers and their heads only visible to him. You squirrels will run up and down his back without being seen,and on hearing this, they giggled together in the trees. Rabbits, all of you will nibble at his legs while you are invisible also.

The rooks and pigeons will save all their poop for one major targeted attack on him when he arrives. There was much squawking and cooing from the trees at that point. Now all this must be done at the same time to ensure that there is the maximum effect, he warned them. We must strike fear into Higginbottom once and for all to save the trees and protect the woodland families.

We need our trees to live and to protect our world also from the poison gases. I have briefed B.G. and all is ready" and with that he stretched his wing over towards B.G.."Thank you, Oldfather said B.G. Now everyone, remember we must wait for Higginbottom to enter into the forest because our magic dust only works while we are in the forest, if we leave the forest it will not work. All the vapours from the trees will help to make the magic dust strong and many of the trees creaked and waved their branches in agreement.

Now you should all break for lunch and directly after lunch the rabbits and squirrels will assist the rooks and pigeons to load up with the magic dust to sprinkle over us. Doeity and I will take a short nap because we have been up all night helping Olfather Owl get ready for this. We will meet up later at 4.30pm over on the south east side of the forest as planned to save Mrs De Blanc s home, her babies and the woodland families living under and in those trees". With that they all slowly departed for lunch chatting among themselves excitedly and side by side they all left.

The lady was so excited, and could hardly believe her eyes and ears. Stumbling off the seat and almost falling onto the tall grass. Dusting herself off,she stood up and looked around. Everyone had gone at this point and so she decided she would go for lunch too back at the hotel and then after lunch find the way to the south east part of the forest to watch what was going to happen.It sounded like a great plan indeed.

# Magic Dust

   Back at the hotel, she felt like she was living a dream. She sat down for a hearty hot lunch of shepherds pie, her favourite dish. She found it hard to concentrate on the food though, because all she could think about was... what had happened in Anderton Forest. Would their plan succeed and would Higginbottom come back at 6pm?, after all he could change his mind and if he did change his plans all B.G.`s efforts and the woodland creatures would be lost. The animals would be so sad and disappointed and maybe they would not be able to save the trees or their homes any more.

   With her map of the forest from the hotel reception spread out on her table while having lunch, she marked her way back. She was a bit surprised when she heard some farmers at the next table mention Higginbottom. She could not concentrate on lunch because all she could think about was the secret happenings in Anderton Forest.

   Would their plan succeed and would Higginbottom go there at six o'clock as the rooks had heard. There was a chance that he might change his mind, she hoped not. If he did change his plans it would be a disaster and spoil the plans. The animals would be sad and maybe they would not be able to do anything to save their forest. But still they all had faith and hope in their plan and that is why she did too.

   Anderton was a huge forest, one of the largest in the Country and maybe the largest in Europe. The views from the front of the hotel were amazing. Looking down over the valley, Anderton forest stretched out as far as the eye could see.

Still she needed to find the correct road that led to the south east part and follow the map along it to see where the tree cutting had started. This would help her to find the right place to view the attack on Mr. Higginbottom.

There were many roads but she marked the route with a pen and decided to set off at 5pm to get there early.

Driving along the twisty winding roads and hoping the directions were correct, she became aware that the time was flying past and it was now almost 5.45 and still she was trying to find the site where the trees were being cut. There were not enough signposts and she had gone down many narrow roads, and taken many wrong turns earlier. About to give up, she decided to continue driving further on with the forest to her left, for a little longer.

Time was passing yet she could not find the tree cutting site. feeling annoyed with herself for not leaving earlier, it was now 6.15 and she was still searching for it.

The when driving around a sharp bend in the road, further up on the hill on the left she saw a bright red tractor parked up. This must be it, she thought excitedly. She parked her car up at the lay by nearby. She got out and started to walk up towards the tractor.

*The Forest Road*

*Higginbottom`s Tractor*

   She checked her watch and remembered what Oldfather had said about the magic dust and wondered if it was still working on the forest animals, but, she didn't need to worry because, the closer she got to the forest entrance, the louder and louder the noises became. There was an enormous uproar of strange animal shrieking and squawking together with loud bellowing noises.

Over the treetops there were hundreds of birds swooping and circling together, diving in and out of the treetops. There were pigeons, rooks and a few hawks. Through all of this noise, the repeated loud screams of a man could be heard. Those screams had to be coming from Higginbottom himself, Just as she hurried up the hill past the tractor, there he was, he came running out of the forest.

   His clothes were ragged and he was covered in bird poop from head to toe and he ran past me screaming loudly. He looked like a sorry sight. Looking after him, as he ran down the road towards his tractor, she could see the back of his green overalls which were well torn almost to shreds by the birds. All down his back was covered in bird poop.

As he ran down the road, he was shouting at her, "stay away from that forest it's haunted I tell you, haunted", he said. "Run while you still can", he shouted from the top of his voice, while waving his hand down the hill. Then he threw something into the back and leaped into the tractor and quickly drove off down the road still screaming back at , her .."get away, get away while you still can".

She stood and watched him disappear down the woodland road leaving a huge pile of dust behind him and waited until the tractor disappeared safely out of sight.

That is the end of Higginbottom`s visits to the forest she said, and still there were loud noises coming from the forest. It must be B.G., Deity and the others, so she decided to go and see what she could find out about their plan.

## The Celebration

Walking quickly back into the forest. It was quieter now, not as noisy as before and she knew the animals would think she could not be seen because of the magic, because Oldfather had said the magic dust would make them all invisible to humans too. So entering the small clearing and there in the middle of the fallen trees was Doeity with B.G. on her back and as she walked closer she could see all the deer, stags, squirrels, rooks, rabbits, badgers and the others jumping and singing for joy. "Well done everyone" shouted B.G. as he sat on Doeity`s back. "Well done, what a great job. "Did you see the look on Higginbottoms face? He was absolutely terrified. I don't think we will be seeing him again" he laughed.

Over on the fallen trees sat two Rabbits hugging. It was Bel de Bouse who was heavily pregnant with her husband who shouted out, "well done everyone and thank you for

32

saving our community, three cheers for B.G... hip hip hooray... hip hip hooray, hip hip hooray". B.G. covered his mouth with his paws appearing slightly embarrassed as he sat on Doeity`s back. "Thank you" he said, "but without us all working together we would not have saved the trees, our homes, and this wonderful forest and you all have played a very important part in saving them and protecting our world, our homes and our families. Trees are magical, trees are magical and not everyone knows this". He said.

  Just then all the branches waved in unison creating a short breeze that nearly blew B.G.`s blue cap off his head. She smiled when she heard him say this, because she always knew trees were magical. " A special thanks to you too, Oldfather Owl" B.G. said. "Please take a bow".

  Just then everyone looked up at the tree, where Oldfather Owl sat, he gracefully stepped forward stretched out a rather large wing then pulled it close to him and bowed over it as he chuckled "too wit too woo to you too" he said. Then all the woodland animals and birds started to chatter among themselves and slowly started making their way back into the forest to their homes while going off in various different directions happily chatting to each other.

  As B.G. was leaving, still sitting on Doeity`s back, he turned right around and looked straight at her, he smiled and shouted "Goodbye lady of the forest" he said waving his paw in her direction, then turned and still on Doeitys back, they continued on and disappeared into the forest.

  She stood there in total surprise. Was there really a lady of the Forest? Did he see her?, or was he looking at someone else?. Was she invisible? Still there were many unanswered questions, but one thing she knew, it was the most amazing day, one she would never forget. Walking back to her car she decided she needed a photo to remember this day.

So she rushed back up the hill and into the woods and took a picture of the place where it had all happened with the fallen trees lying on the ground amid the yellow, white and blue wild flowers and green grasses and also a decent splash of bird poop dotted all around. The sun shone in through trees to brighten up the scene. It was so quiet now as all the animals had disappeared. She sat down to rest on the log and noticed B.G.'s cap had blown off and was resting on the log, or did he leave it there for her?. She put it safely in her bag, and promised to return it to him directly, the next time she visited. She was happy the plan turned out to be such a great success and those brave woodland creatures had succeeded in helping to save their forest and in doing that they had also helped to make Anderton Forest a safe place and this had made her holiday there simply unforgettable.

When she got back to London she printed out the photo which now stands in a shiny silver frame on her office desk. So whenever she gets stressed with city life, she looks at the photo of B.G.'s small blue cap resting on top of one of the fallen trees and remembers one of the Secrets of Anderton Forest.

The End.

## The Office Photo – B.G.`s Blue Cap.

# A Message From Anderton Forest

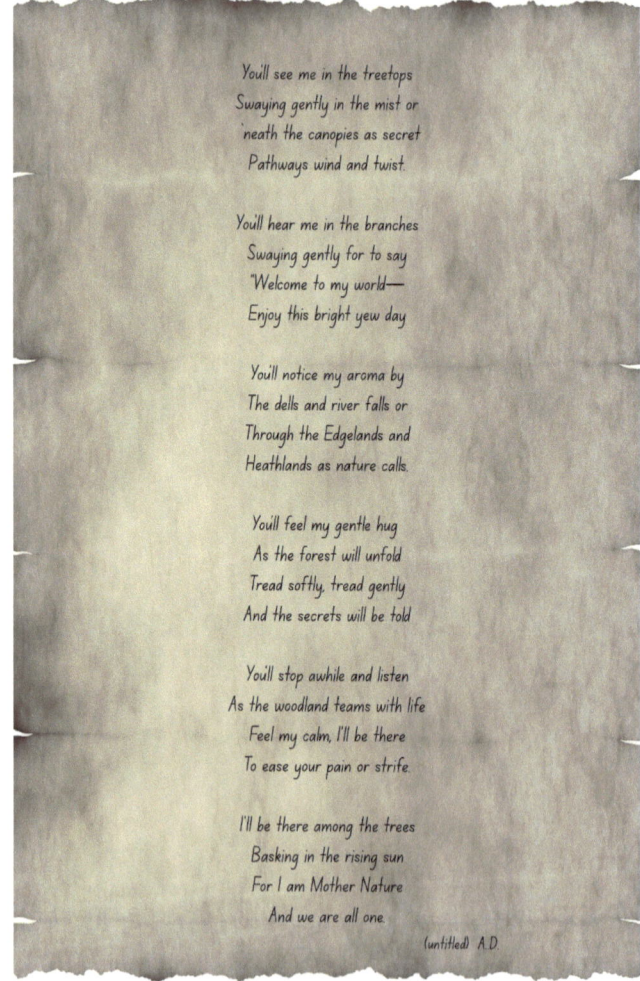

You'll see me in the treetops
Swaying gently in the mist or
'neath the canopies as secret
Pathways wind and twist.

You'll hear me in the branches
Swaying gently for to say
"Welcome to my world—
Enjoy this bright yew day

You'll notice my aroma by
The dells and river falls or
Through the Edgelands and
Heathlands as nature calls.

You'll feel my gentle hug
As the forest will unfold
Tread softly, tread gently
And the secrets will be told

You'll stop awhile and listen
As the woodland teams with life
Feel my calm, I'll be there
To ease your pain or strife.

I'll be there among the trees
Basking in the rising sun
For I am Mother Nature
And we are all one.

(untitled) A.D.

(untitled).

# Forest References

**Guardians:**
Those who protect things.

**Beak-writers:**
A special skill to write with ones beak.

**Extraordinary General Meeting:**
A very unusual and special meeting

**Meeting Minutes:**
Notes taken at important meetings.

**Bark Wood:**
The outer layer of wood on a tree trunk

**Forest Inks:**
Found in oak leaves, blackberries and elderberries.

**Wisdom Book Records & Magic:**
A special book which records important messages and magic

**.Good Wisdom Wizardry:**
A person dedicated to magic for the good of others.

LOOK OUT FOR SECRET TWO....
COMING SOON:

SECRETS IN ANDERTON FOREST
.
"QUILLTON`S URGENT PIGEON POST"

## Copyright Notice:

All rights reserved, no part of this publication may be reproduced, stored in a retrieval system, or transmitted in any form or by any means- electronic, mechanical, photocopying, recording, or otherwise – without the prior written permission of the author.

ISBN (Print):979-8-89965-952-2

ISBN (eBook): 979-8-89965-0

This is a work of fiction. Any resemblance to real persons, living or dead, or to actual places is purely coincidental.

© 2025 A.Daly.

*"A Protect The Trees Initiative"*

# Secrets in Anderton Forest

## *An Extraordinary General Meeting*

## *A. Daly.*

*Book one in the Secrets in Anderton Forest Series*

*Thank You for Reading!*

www.ingramcontent.com/pod-product-compliance
Lightning Source LLC
Chambersburg PA
CBHW040949050426
42337CB00048B/58